Songs of Love

Songs of Love

Kevin Pakenham

First published in Great Britain in 2020 by
Bernhurst Press

Edited, designed and produced by Tandem Publishing
http://tandempublishing.yolasite.com

ISBN: 978-1-5272-7005-3

10 9 8 7 6 5 4 3 2 1

A CIP catalogue record for this book is available from the British Library.

Printed and bound in Great Britain by CPI Group (UK) Ltd, Croydon CR0 4YY.

Dedicated:

To my sister Judith Kazantzis

Acknowledgements:

All who have travelled the stormy seas, and particularly my wife Ronke who has mastered the swell.

Songs of Love

Drawings

As they appear

Hurlingham
Judith's Funeral
From Matisse
From Utamaro
Fairlight
From Manet One
From Manet Two
Thurlestone
Spare Room
Bernhurst

Contents

Songs of Innocence

Contents continued

Songs of Experience

Songs of Innocence

L'Impasse des Deux Anges

I came on an impasse, an impulse of angels,
I asked them politely to unblock my way,
They laughed and they sighed and they jostled
each other
Replied with a glint, how much would I pay.

"What can I give you, what feeble endearment,
What breath of my spirit can match your
array?
For you in the heavens, with armfuls of star
buds,
I am a poor human with nothing to say."

I took a step forward, and found I am back
And spinning, a dust speck, wherever it may,
And far in the impasse an impulse of laughter,
"Come on little human, come over and play."

After You'd Gone

After you'd gone,
I found your knickers in the bed,
Black and silky and sweet and mine,
And your knickers too.
They smelt so sweet of you.

And I thought, as I put them to my lips,
Suppose, just suppose,
(I'm brave enough to think this,
Savour it, hold it,
Only because it's not)
Just suppose, suppose,
I were never ever to see you
Again.

You see what I mean?
You'd have gone.
What then would I do,
With those black sweet silky knickers,
That smell of you, that you,
What then would I do?

Cry like a baby in their silky
folds?
Tear them apart, as you'd be
torn from me?
Rant at them, abuse them,
stamp them inside out?
No my darling, no.
I'd stare just at them blankly.
And put them carefully,
Carefully into the bin.
Then, with steady head,
Climb in there too.

Up in the Powder

I've got a red devil who sits on my shoulder,
The jolliest chap you ever would meet,
With a long pointed tail and a load of the
blarney,
"Oh, Kevin, my fellah, your skiing is greet."

On a quality piste when the sun is so brightly
Flashing the buckles and raising the heat,
My little admirer sits there on my shoulder
And silkily whispers, "You're skiing a treat.
"Why don't you go faster? Go up in the
powder,
"Show us your tricks, lad, there's none you
can't beat!
"Oh, look at your movements, so fine and so
lithesome,
"You are just terrific, my fellah, my mate!"

So where are you now, my little red devil?
Why have you left me alone in this bed?
My foot in a plaster, my arm in a bandage
And fed by a drip that goes into my head,
Why have you left me, when most I need
cheering?
Why have you scarpered and left me for dead?

Outward Bound

Wishing with the engines
At thirty thousand feet,
In blind determination
I'm stretched upon the seat.
The plane is bound for Singapore
And I am bound there too,
But it really would be better
To be bound in bed with you.

Oh Mountain Sea!

Oh mountain sea you're not for me!
With whiten caps and slabs of sound,
Don't fall upon this human prey,
Lost beneath a cloak of spray.
Go! Hurtle to the bare horizon,
To another mariner, another nothing mariner,
Go crack and slap and undermine
With frightful energy and mass,
And thumping through the underground,
The flesh and bones you slap and crack,
Oh leave me be! Oh leave me be!
Go crush another mariner, a nothing ever
mariner,
Oh leave me be! Oh leave me be!
I do not need you mountain sea.

An Episode

An episode came through the door
And tempted me to make a date.
It lay upon the bedroom floor.
I came at once, not to be late.

The episode was satisfied,
And so was I, I'm glad to say –
We like a little on the side
And hope there's nothing more to pay.

But when the wind in winter trees
Strips back the episode again,
The touch of yesterday will tease
And test anew my aching pen.

When flecks of rain upon that wind
Mix tears from lashes on my cheek,
And show that I am un-resigned –
An episode I did not seek,

Will then the heat, the bedroom floor,
Flow back to me, my Ariel?
And find that through a private door
The episode was serial.

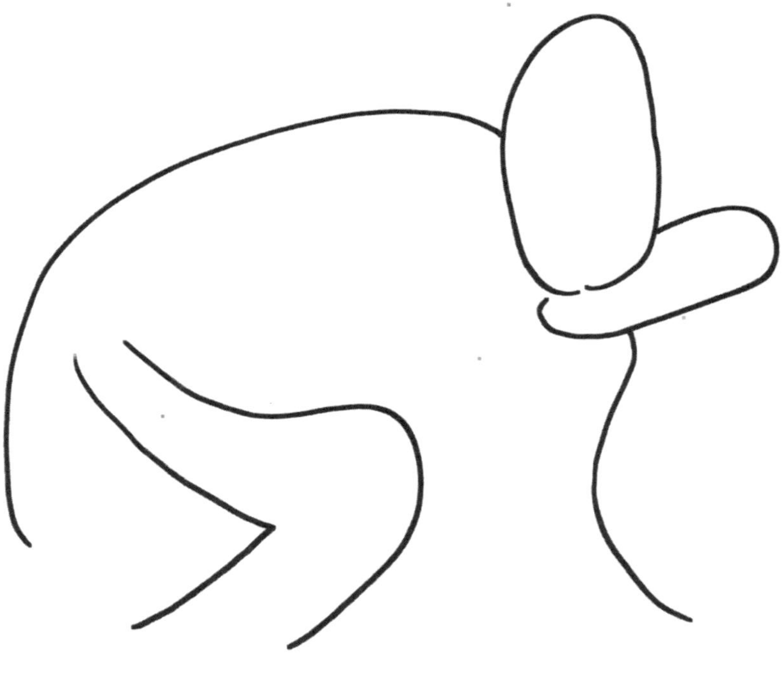

Lichtenstein to Wittgenstein

In the instant, in the moment,
In the twinkle of an eye
When my root is rooted in you,
When my thigh is on your thigh,
When my tuft is tufted to you,
When your sigh is with my sigh.

In the instant I'm upon you,
In the moment here and now,
That moment always coming,
Always passing, always now,

In that twinkle, in that tinkle,
In the wrinkling of time,
And I hear the glasses breaking,
And I hear our calling chime,

In the well that I am plumbing,
In that boiling that is you,
And I'm bursting like a piston
As the train comes clattering through,

In that lightning, in that thunder,
In the storm of here and now,
Like a pirate on his plunder
With my crashing and Kerpow!

That Kerpow! That Kerpow?
Was it really then? Or now?
And how was it then?

Tell me how.
And who? Tell me who.
And you, was it you?
Was it you?

The Green Sea

"I saw you slip silently into the green sea"
But the sea was mist grey, sun blue, yellow
sand.
"I saw you slip silently into the green sea,
I held the image in my right hand."
I was alone on the waves so frisky,
We chomped at the bit of the cantering waves,
And over the transom the white horse skipped,
And whinnied and stomped as we made our
way.
"I saw you slip silently into the green sea,
I held the image in the palm of my hand"
Round and round in the palm of your hand,
A wandering finger which followed me down,
"No listen, no listen you must understand,
I saw you slip silently into the green sea"
Yes, yes I remember, into the green sea
Into the mist grey,
Into the sun blue
In the beige sand.

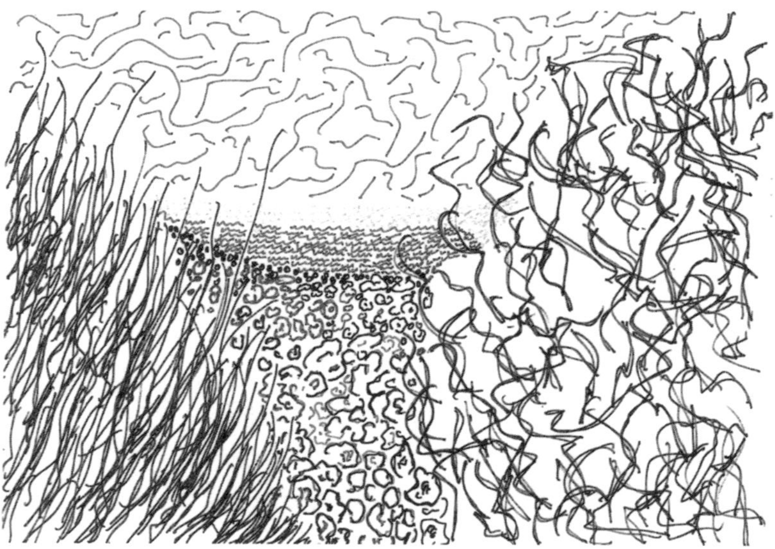

At Sea

The strap of a spa, a clip, a hook,
The brimming head, the heaving wave,
The sigh of the sea and a whispering look,
Her starfish limbs she pulls away.
The surge behind and the hands between,
The threatening sky and the sea bird call,
The toss of the mane with face unseen,
The buck of the hips, the rise and fall.
The foaming surge on the sloping walls,
The wet salt wrack and the sheeting spume,
The smash of the roller breaking hard
Dragging her up in a sea green plume.
Plunging down in the darkening blue,
Up to the hilt in the gully deep,
The screaming wind above her cries,
Heel over head in a crescent sweep.
Poised on the edge, on the ridge of time,
Hanging across, on the pivot spa,
The oh! of her lips are ringed with rime,
She drums to the beat of the ocean bar.

My Picture of You

I thought today of a polaroid camera
Specially bought to capture you,
In every position that God ever thought of,
And a few.

I thought of every part I'd capture
With care and dedication true,
And how you, and gravity would help me
To worship you.

I'd worship you like a dancing Zulu,
Club up high and blazing eyes,
My cries and calls of admiration
To appeal to you.

I'd worship you as a kneeling Christian,
With a holy gaze upon your you,
And pray for the force of the inner spirit
To transport you.

I'd worship you as an intellectual
And find a logical fit for you,
And tie myself in threads of reason
As a gift for you.

But most of all I'd worship you
To make you a Goddess through and through,
And when you're a Goddess all the way
through,
I'd have taken you.

Gone to the Gula Gula

Across the floor, the samba school,
Bottoms swirl and breasts are smacking
Degrees advance past boiling pointment
Drenched in love and unguent ointment –
Every heart is clack clack clacking!
The drum of midriff, double footed
Stuffing strutted,
Sweeping rain through sweat, cerveza,
Slipping sliding to the beating –
Black and brown and twinkling piggies,
All are pounding, no retreating –
Buttocks clashing, breasts are rolling
Arms and hands are thrown in ether,
Far beyond all human hearing!
Beating, beating, samba beating!
Ecstasy is nearing, nearing!
Love and lust are tearing, tearing!
Far beyond all hope or fearing!
Gone! Gone! Gone! To the Gula Gula!
Gone to the world of the samba school.

On the Prow

My friend curly loves to stand,
On the prow, on the prow.
My friend curly holds his hand
And shows you how, he shows you how.
The clear cool waters part before
And gliding through the blue black depths,
He takes your hand and offers more,
A little twist, a pussy paw,
And you can slowly ask for more,
A bit before, a bit before.

My friend curly loves to stand,
And hold the water in his hand.
He loves to feel the waters part
That beat and bustle to your heart.
He loves to see you turn and twist
And hear the music through the mist,
And in your eyes plunge every depth,
Until he's left, until he's left
You out of breath, out of breath.

Swimming in Singapore

In the palm of my hand
Two coconuts fell,
Ah – bunch – lunge – glide,
Shlop – shlop – ooh – shlop,
Into the sweaty palms,
Smooth as malacca,
The hairy coconuts fell,
And nestled there.
I weighed them and
Smelled the coconut oil.
Soft – warm – gliding – sweet,
Shlop – shlop – ooh – shlop.
Kerlunk went the water –
Side to side,
Side to side –
And I thought it, spilled
From the cracked nuts,
Onto the swimming pool side.

My Palm on Your Cheek

As pad of a cat, stealthy over the roof,
My hand finds your cheek,
Resting its paw, its fur on your skin
With a purr.
My palm swells and falls
With your breath from deep,
Heart beats softly, sweetly, pulsing through
My palm, your cheek.

"Hold me" it says, "hold me,
"Come to my places you've never been,
"Places for me of quiet and peace,
"Away, away from all that hangs heavy on me,
"Weighs heavy, heavy hanging weights.
"I feel your palm,
"Your palm on my cheek,
"Your palm moulded to the folds of my cheek.
"The bird rests nestling, steady in the crevice
        of the boughs,
"Of the sheltering trees."

Breathing more deeply, more slowly, sweetly,
Turning your head on the pillow,
Your cheek melting to my palm,
And drifting with the sweet balm,
Settled in soft blissful sleep.

The Boy on the Bridge

The boy on the bridge drops a stone in
the water,
He watches the ripples as they disappear.
"Am I a ripple?" he asks of the water,
"Is it a ripple that's keeping me here?"
"Yes" said the water "you are but a
ripple,
"You cannot be more, you cannot be
less,
"And here in my depths you shall never
stop beating,
"Feeling the love of a mother's caress."

Songs of Experience

Burnt Out under Hastings Pier

No Houdini I,
A packing case man,
A rat, dislocated jaw and all.
Dislocated. I lie.
Above – slatted rain sweeps teeth, burnt rotten.
Below – thump, thump, thump,
Pull and suck, pull and suck.

Once a thousand trips of beating hearts,
The swish and turn of spruce and ordered
steps,
White tuxedos yet,
On boards, diagonal, patterned, parquet,
Shining to a fault.
And ladies' room, a fret of powder, sweat and
thrill.
A few short steps to sitting-out, a grope, a nip,
a tuck,
A surge to match the surge below
New and fresh,
New, and forged from an old pattern.

Below – a fugitive I crouch.
One eye down – the cold green waters do not
give.
One eye up – through cracks I see

Trouser legs, leather on my cheek,
And between the sharp stilettoes,
I glimpse the gussets and the bows,
The gartered thighs,
The belts suspensive,
The pink satin fringed with curly black,
Expectant, panting to see the vista of a black
        forest,
A gateau veritable.
To see but not to smell, no taste, no shock,
They whirl away,
And my eye down is dowsed –
The plunging sea, the pull and suck,
Battering the great dark poles, that hold me up,
Precarious.

Kerlunk, kerlunk, clatter.
Rattling joy of dirty metal in a child's hand,
A winning streak but far from home.
Kerlunk, kerlunk, clatter.
The one armed bandit gives a tug,
More enjoyable, more reliable
Another torrent of dirty coppers fall
Into the battered tray.

Merrily, merrily, shall I live now?
Where is the blossom that hung on the bow?

No Houdini, do not cry,
Beneath the floor boards here I lie,
Though the sea is cold and bleak,
And the dancing? Do not speak.
Still within this space I breathe,
Kiss me once and take your leave.

A Cathedral of Transport

On Sunday PM Gare du Nord,
The virgin and the unicorn
Rub shoulders with returning whore –
Where is the sword of truth and love?
Whose is the cry of soul replete?
Can they swear by what's above,
From rolling stock to tired feet,
That they have lived their destiny,
In rolls of fat,
In slabs of lard,
Or held the present in their hands,
Where cappuccino or a monk,
Both soft and frothing in their cups,
May find repose or never wake?
And will they answer when they're called
By greater natures than their own,
From this cathedral of delight?

The Flagmen

The flagmen come in crinkled ranks
Across the thighs of Sussex downs,
They crack their poles upon the flanks
Of flying feet and feathered gowns.

The cry of hawk and bark of fox
Are echoed by the smack of cloth,
And stripped aside are hens and cocks
As deadly spit the guns of wrath.

The shafts of lead stream to the beak
And crunch on bone and beating wing –
The strain of butt on fleshy cheek
Loves jolt and jug as barrels sing.

The wheeling flagmen whip the sky
In answer to the chant of lead,
And boot on clump will clump on by
As earth resounds to quick and dead.

The welt of down! The round of combe
Enfold in curl of glacial sweep
Embrace the alabaster tomb –
But still these deadly passions keep.

Love in Venice

Upon the balcony, before the balustrade,
Beneath the curve of Moorish architrave
Here, centuries of lovers stand,
Some sad, some true, some unbetrayed.
In flowing night gown, half revealing all,
In manly pose and boyish smirk,
In flowered hat and nothing more,
In harsh tuxedo, ready for the ball.
Before the balustrade they flow,
Bowing on this little stage,
Their wishes knotted tight between their legs,
A paroxysm then away, they go.

Turning Turtle

Once I, the new hatched turtle,
Scratched in the sand for food.
Smooth, shelter of carapace, shining in
        the moon,
Soft and tender, so soon unyolked,
My fine formed legs began
The long scrabble with life.

Today my large scoops
Move ponderous and slow,
As with the stately weight of time
My huge encrusted dome,
Across the floor of ageless seascape
        crawls,
Carries my past and all its dying weight.

Come deep sea breaker, rolling on,
Come tidal wave, come hurricane, come
        all,
Come Krakatoa from your sleep,
Take all my past
And crack it on the shore.

The Henge by Moonlight

Seeing you again,
Like a distant toy
In a once loved nursery,
(Slow afternoons on hands and knees
        on the carpeted floor)
Pass by –
(A moment by moonlight,
Pillars of stone)
You, as you then were,
Come back unbroken.

Eclipse at Rye

I shall tell the tale of my eclipse –
How, on that morning, slipped
The bubbling fingers of Earth's desire,
Caressing the soft, slimy banks
In shivers of curling, waiting pants,
Enveloping, lifting, embracing,
Our waiting hull.

The ropes pulled against the cleats
And I felt our platform deck
Shudder. The keel was levered off
The warm holding banks,
Till with a surge –
"Let go the ropes – let go!"
And we were cast to flow
Down the sinuous channel,
Down to the welcoming sea
On that Summer's morning.

Behind, the citadel glints,
Knobby in the risen sun,
And all is warmed and glows,
Rocking to the gentle surf,
Down the estuary of ease, sweet ease,
We go.

Beat on, our large white wings,
Huge handkerchiefs, tied billowing
To our masterful mast.
Sun, so bright and confident,
Sun, hard on our faces,
Pulling us on, cocksure,
Our jaws set and eyes diamantine,
In that morning.
I tell the tale of my eclipse.

We knew it was coming,
We were ready for it, for
The wind, and the dark and
The horrible loss –
And the moon, black moon,
A huge dark hole over our sun,
Our very own sun mocked,
Mocked in its own sky,
And the water was up and we were down,
Cast down,
And the sun was a sliver,
A poor weak sliver,
Behind a huge gaping hole
Through a chiffon of cloud.

Pop – the shout of champagne –
A pop, little pop, and a fizz,
And a spew, and a phew, and –

Our spirits rose as it spluttered out –
"Phew" we said, "That's better".
It was for a time, short time, too short time,
Only one pop, one fizz.

Then our sails filled with a great gust,
The ropes pulled tight
And the light was thin
As old man's urine –
We were bruised and buffeted to nowhere,
In double quick time.

Hello, old sun,
Nice to see you back,
But you went, you know –
You left us alone,
Alone to the black hole
Of an old wench.

Moon over Mount Fuji

I saw the moon rise, through the kitchen floor,
Between the grey stone flags, I saw you rise,
You were no different from you were before,
An angel of paradise, a faithful whore,
You rise.
You are no different from you were before,
Your loves, your memories, your all,
They are no different from they were before,
The blood is crimson from the neck and more,
But you, Oh moon, have seen it all before,
Between the cracks, upon the kitchen floor.

On Brightling Hill

On Brightling Hill a trig point in the Weald,
A finger pointing at the puffy sky,
Sits old man Fuller,
Mad Jack his nom de guerre,
A rictus grin amidst his bones now dry.
The wind wriggles through the dark yew halls
And still old Jack expectant waits
His pentagonal summoning.
Ears long gone,
Wisps of hair still straggle down,
And he uncocked but waiting –
An irrational gamble on the last trump.

You Lent me the Key to your Heart

You lent me the key to your heart.
I held it, a thing apart,
And weighted it in my palm –
Three keys to be precise,
One for each part.

The first:
To come from the noisy street,
The barge and shove of busy feet,
Into your ante-room of calm.

Then up the stairs,
My heart beating, my legs pumping,
The oxygen thinning.

I reach the summit,
          Slip in one,
          Slip in two.
I'm through.

A final step by step,
A teeter on the edge,
A moment more,
A fold of cloth,
A button and a bow,
A wiggle from above

And one below,
A sigh, a cry,
No heart no beat,
When all is not,
Will it? Will it not?
        I slip in you.

You lent me the key to your heart.
But now you have called it in.
Here it is – just as it was.
It was yours to take back.
A loan repaid, a bond now slipped.

Its shadow rests on my heart,
A thing apart,
Which you slipped me,
And I slipped back,
And still it slips, where it once slipped,
With me, in my heart.

Venice in Winter

Along the Dorsoduro, where the barges moan,
There I met a young girl, all alone,
Her breasts were sweet as marmalade,
And her eyes shone,
Her legs went up the campanile,
And were gone.

Let You Hear My Voice

When you roll, enclosed, within the bearish
arms
That carry you, a bear cub, to his bed,
As he, in tones familiar,
Sweet talks your fears away,
You, in the peace of the pelt of your ursine
couch,
That gently rumbles, rocks you to repose –
Then, like a whisper on an Alpine slope,
When slabs of snow lie balanced on the craggy
granite sheets,
Then in whispers, only whispers,
As a distant pipe of Pan,
Those whispers growing to distant groans and
creaks,
Growing to drum of moving snow,
To thunderous rumble of your moving world
At last, astounded:
The chandelier of stars comes crashing
through
Unhinging all –
The butterfly beat of an alien voice.

Our Pleasures

Last night I wondered where you were,
Within whose arms last night you lay,
Against whose chest, against whose hair
You laid your breasts until the day.

Can you remember, long ago,
When in your heart my love lay
    locked?
And how by kisses I could show
Your heart by tremors daily rocked?

Or do you dare to think about
The plans we made, the days we
    spent?
And in my heart I did not doubt
The words we said we really meant.

In age and sense our days now pass,
We seek ourselves in other eyes,
And now to both our words are farce,
For newer sense the body cries.

Tonight I think of you once more,
As hour by hour the minutes run,
Is this what we a living for?
To take our pleasures one by one?

And Your Life Goes On

A child's kiss upon my cheek,
A friendly pat upon his head,
The radio voice repeats itself,
And your life goes on.

The morning rain is dropping out,
The car begins at second turn,
I put my jacket on the seat,
And your life goes on.

I call the East, I call the West,
I call a meeting in my room,
I write a memo, copied round,
And your life goes on.

I walk along the River Thames,
I lunch on sole and Chardonnay,
I take my coat and tip the girl,
And your life goes on.

I sit and watch the sunlight fade,
And watch the tide flow out to sea,
With all the dreams of those that wait,
And your life goes on.

I am alone tonight, alone
In the cavern of my thoughts,
Frozen in my consequence,
And your life goes on.

With You

On the edge of the meadow
In the short grass,
Under the willow tree,
With the smell of the earth and
    the vetch,
Shared with the thrush and the bee.

On the moss in the clearing
Under the soaring pines,
Hugging and warm,
With the clouds touching
The pricks of the crowns of the
    huge parasol.

With the sound of the stream
Over the pebbles and rocks,
And the irises wide,
With their blue and their yellow,
The water a bed.

In the dell in the snow,
A miracle dimple of light,
A cocoon of delight,
Under the crags
Of the roof of the world.

In the lapping of waves
At the end of the swell,
Lying but standing,
Floating on sand –
The seabirds a chorus of joy.

In each of these glories of earth
You deserve to receive
Like a gift of Apollo,
A lover with limbs and with tongue
Of every elaborate perfection
This glorious planet can show.

And as you explode and recoup
And embrace and reflect
And hold in your being the cascade
of light
That comes from within
and without,
And will endlessly flow
In all this extravagant gift
That your body provides

Then I shall rejoice to be there,
At the moment of all,
The green flash of light,
The music of spheres,

As all in your mind and your body
    is one –
Then, wherever you are,
In the meadow, the moss or the stream,

The dell in the snow or the lapping
    of waves,
Whomever you take to your breast,
And your heart and your soul,
It is I.